GOD IS EVER NEW

POPE BENEDICT XVI

God Is Ever New

*Meditations on Life, Love,
and Freedom*

With a Foreword by
Pope Francis

Edited by Luca Caruso

IGNATIUS PRESS   SAN FRANCISCO

Original text:
Dio è sempre nuovo
© 2023, Dicastero per la Comunicazione—
Libreria Editrice Vaticana, Vatican City

Cover art: Photograph of Pope Benedict XVI
and his papal coat of arms
by Stefano Spaziani

Cover design by Roxanne Mei Lum

Published in 2024 by Ignatius Press, San Francisco
Foreword © 2024 by Ignatius Press, San Francisco
All rights reserved
ISBN 978-1-62164-652-5 (HB)
ISBN 978-1-64229-283-1 (eBook)
Library of Congress Control Number 2023947045
Printed in the United States of America ∞

CONTENTS

God's Yes Is Stronger Than All of Us
Meditations on Faith

The Love That Comes from God Is Eternal
Meditations on Love

Praying Is Human, Because God Is Human
Meditations on Prayer

We Are Made for Eternity
Meditations for Young People and Families

Trust Joyfully in God's Promises
Meditations on Hope

All Is Grace, Not Something "I Did"
Meditations on Holiness

We Find Life Only in Giving It
Meditations on Truth and Freedom

Loved, Therefore Happy
Meditations on Joy

FOREWORD

By Pope Francis

I am overjoyed that the reader can hold in his hands this book of spiritual meditations by the late Pope Benedict XVI. Already the title expresses one of the most distinctive aspects of my predecessor's teaching and vision of the faith: yes, *God is ever new*, because he is the source and reason of beauty, grace, and truth. God is never repetitious—God surprises us; God brings newness. The freshness of spirit radiating from these pages emphatically confirms this.

Benedict XVI did theology on his knees. In discussing and debating the faith, he showed the devotion of a man who had surrendered his whole self to God and who, guided by the Holy Spirit, sought an ever fuller interpenetration with the mystery of Jesus—the same Jesus who had enthralled him since childhood.

This collection shows Benedict XVI's creative capacity to probe the many aspects of Christianity with a richness of image, language, and perspective that continually prompts us to cultivate the precious gift of being able to welcome God into our lives. Benedict XVI knew how to bring heart and mind, thought and feeling, rationality and emotion in concert with one another—a fruitful

Foreword translated by Thomas Jacobi, Ignatius Press.

model of how one can tell the world about the shattering power of the Gospel.

The reader will see this at work in these pages, which—under the skilled editorial pen of Luca Caruso, whom we thank heartily—serve as a kind of "spiritual synthesis" of the writings of Benedict XVI. Shining forth in this collection is the late pope's capacity to reveal the depth of the Christian faith in all its newness. With him, just one little phrase is enough. "God is an event of love": a single sentence that does full justice to a theology wherein reason and feeling are ever in harmony.[1] "What could ever save us apart from love?" he asked a group of young people at a 2005 prayer vigil in Cologne (a meditation rightly included in this volume), posing a question that echoes Russian novelist Fyodor Dostoyevsky.[2] And when Benedict XVI speaks of the Church, his ecclesial passion energizes his words more than ever with a sense of belonging and affection: "We are not a production plant, we are not a for-profit business, we are Church."[3]

The profundity of Joseph Ratzinger's thought, founded on Sacred Scripture and on the Fathers of the Church, is still helpful for us today. This collection addresses around twenty different spiritual themes and can stimulate us to remain open to the horizon of eternity that is built into the very DNA of Christianity.

---

[1] Homily at the Solemn Mass of Pentecost, Meeting with the Ecclesial Movements and New Communities, Vatican City (June 3, 2006).

[2] Address at World Youth Day Vigil, Cologne (August 20, 2005).

[3] Benedict XVI with Peter Seewald, *Light of the World: The Pope, the Church, and the Signs of the Times*, trans. Michael J. Miller and Adrian J. Walker (San Francisco: Ignatius Press, 2010), 73.

The thought and teaching of Benedict XVI are and will always be fruitful within time, because he focused on the fundamental reference points for our Christian lives: above all, the Person and the words of Jesus Christ, as well as the theological virtues of love, hope, and faith. And for this the Church will be grateful. Forever.

In Benedict XVI, an unceasing devotion and a luminous teaching are welded together in a harmonious alliance. How many times he spoke of beauty with such moving words! Benedict always considered beauty a privileged road for opening men and women to the transcendent and thus to an encounter with God; for him, this was the highest task and the most urgent mission of the Church. Music was particularly close to his heart, an art form that elevated the spirit and the inner man. But this did not distract his attention—man of faith as he was—from the great, thorny questions of our time, which he observed and analyzed with a conscious judgment and a courageous critical spirit. By listening to the Scriptures, read in the ever lively tradition of the Church, he knew from his youth how to draw from their practical, indispensable wisdom to set up a dialogue with the culture of his own time, as these pages show.

We thank God for giving us Pope Benedict XVI. Through his word and his witness, he taught us that with reflection, thought, study, listening, dialogue, and above all prayer, it is possible to serve the Church and to do good to all mankind. He left us with fine intellectual tools that allow every believer to give a reason for his hope, with a mode of thinking and communicating that can be understood by our own age. Benedict's intention was constant: to enter into dialogue with all people so that they might seek together the roads by which man can come to an encounter with God.

Joseph Ratzinger always had a burning desire for this sort of dialogue with the culture of his own time. As a theologian and then as a shepherd, he never confined himself to a realm of intellectual knowledge, disincarnate and abstracted from the story of man and of the world. An intellectual full of love and enthusiasm (which etymologically means "to be in God"), he showed us through example that it is possible to seek after the truth and that letting yourself be possessed by this truth is a goal far beyond the reach of the human mind. Along this path, all the dimensions of man—reason, faith, intelligence, and spirituality—have their own role and their own specific place.

Benedict XVI taught us by word and example that the fullness of our existence can be found only in a personal encounter with Jesus Christ, the Living One, the incarnate Logos, the full and definitive revelation of God, who from beginning to end is manifested as Love.

My wish is that the reader might find in these pages—which resound with the meek and passionate voice of a great teacher of faith and hope—the grace of a new, life-giving encounter with Jesus.

Vatican, January 3, 2023

Francesco

To Let Him Find Us

Meditations on God and Jesus

Wherever Jesus Is, People Change

There are many things that we do not see, but they exist and are essential. For example: we do not see our reason, yet we have reason. We do not see our intelligence, and we have it. In a word: we do not see our soul, and yet it exists and we see its effects, because we can speak, think, and make decisions, etc. Nor do we see an electric current, for example, yet we see that it exists; we see this microphone, that it is working, and we see lights. Therefore, we do not see the very deepest things, those that really sustain life and the world, but we can see and feel their effects. This is also true for electricity; we do not see the electric current, but we see the light. So it is with the Risen Lord: we do not see him with our eyes, but we see that wherever Jesus is, people change, they improve. A greater capacity for peace, for reconciliation, etc., is created. Therefore, we do not see the Lord himself, but we see the effects of the Lord: so we can understand that Jesus is present.

And as I said, it is precisely the invisible things that are the most profound, the most important. So let us go to meet this invisible but powerful Lord who helps us to live well.

Meeting with Children after Their First Communion, October 15, 2005

We Fall into God's Good Hands

This world of ours is a world of fear: the fear of misery and poverty, the fear of illness and suffering, the fear of solitude, the fear of death. We have in this world a widely developed insurance system; it is good that it exists. But we know that at the moment of deep suffering, at the moment of the ultimate loneliness of death, no insurance policy will be able to protect us. The only valid insurance in those moments is the one that comes to us from the Lord, who also assures us: "Do not fear, I am always with you." We can fall, but in the end we fall into God's hands, and God's hands are good hands.

Homily at the Holy Mass, Church of Santa Maria Consolatrice, Rome, December 18, 2005

God Matters

It seems to me that the great challenge of our time ...
is secularization: that is, a way of living and presenting
the world as "si Deus non daretur", in other words, as
if God did not exist. There is a desire to reduce God to
the private sphere, to a sentiment, as if he were not an
objective reality. As a result, everyone makes his own
plan of life. But this vision, presented as though it were
scientific, accepts as valid only what can be proven.
With a God who is not available for immediate experi-
mentation, this vision ends by also injuring society. The
result is in fact that each one makes his own plan and in
the end finds himself opposed to the other. As can be
seen, this is definitely an unlivable situation. We must
make God present again in our society. This seems to
me to be the first essential element: that God be once
again present in our lives, that we do not live as though
we were autonomous, authorized to invent what freedom and life are. We must realize that we are creatures,
aware that there is a God who has created us and that
living in accordance with his will is not dependence but
a gift of love that makes us alive.

Therefore, the first point is to know God, to know
him better and better, to recognize that God is in my life
and that God matters.... The second point, therefore,

is recognizing God, who has shown us his face in Jesus, who suffered for us, who loved us to the point of dying, and thus overcame violence. It is necessary to make the living God present in our "own" lives first of all, the God who is not a stranger, a fictitious God, a God only thought of, but a God who has shown himself, who has shown his being and his face. Only in this way do our lives become true, authentically human; hence, the criteria of true humanism emerge in society.... We cannot be alone in building this just and righteous life but must journey on in the company of good and upright friends, companions with whom we can experience that God exists and that it is beautiful to walk with God and to walk in the great company of the Church, which presents to us down the centuries God, who speaks, who acts, who accompanies us. Therefore, I would say: find God, find God revealed in Jesus Christ, walk in company with his great family, with our brothers and sisters who are God's family.

Meeting with the Youth of Rome and Lazio for World Youth Day, April 6, 2006

God Is Love, Not Mathematical Reason

God exists, or he does not exist. There are only two options. Either one recognizes the priority of reason, of creative Reason that is at the beginning of all things and is the principle of all things—the priority of reason is also the priority of freedom—or one holds the priority of the irrational, inasmuch as everything that functions on our earth and in our lives would be only accidental, marginal, an irrational result—reason would be a product of irrationality. One cannot ultimately "prove" either project, but the great option of Christianity is the option for rationality and for the priority of reason. This seems to me to be an excellent option, which shows us that behind everything is a great Intelligence to which we can entrust ourselves.

However, the true problem challenging faith today seems to me to be the evil in the world: we ask ourselves how it can be compatible with the Creator's rationality. And here we truly need God, who was made flesh and shows us that he is not only a mathematical reason but that this original Reason is also Love. If we look at the great options, the Christian option today is the one that is the most rational and the most human. Therefore, we can confidently work out a philosophy, a vision of the world based on this priority of reason, on this trust that the creating Reason is love and that this love is God.

Meeting with the Youth of Rome and Lazio for World Youth Day, April 6, 2006

In the Absence of God,
There Are Questions concerning Him

A God who is merely imagined and invented is not God at all. If he does not reveal himself, we cannot gain access to him. The novelty of Christian proclamation is that it can now say to all peoples: he has revealed himself. He personally. And now the way to him is open. The novelty of Christian proclamation does not consist in a thought, but in a deed: God has revealed himself. Yet this is no blind deed, but one which is itself *Logos*— the presence of eternal reason in our flesh. *Verbum caro factum est* (Jn 1:14): just so, amid what is made (*factum*), there is now *Logos*; *Logos* is among us. Creation (*factum*) is rational. Naturally, the humility of reason is always needed, in order to accept it: man's humility, which responds to God's humility.

Our present situation differs in many respects from the one that Paul encountered in Athens, yet despite the difference, the two situations also have much in common. Our cities are no longer filled with altars and with images of multiple deities. God has truly become for many the great unknown. But just as in the past, when behind the many images of God the question concerning the unknown God was hidden and present, so, too, the present absence of God is silently besieged by the question concerning him. *Quaerere Deum*—to seek God and to let oneself be found by him, that is today no less necessary than in former times. A purely positivistic culture that tried to drive the question concerning God into the subjective realm, as being unscientific, would be the capitulation of reason, the renunciation of its highest possibilities, and hence a disaster for humanity, with very grave consequences. What gave Europe's culture its foundation—the search for God and the readiness to listen to him—remains today the basis of any genuine culture.

Meeting at the Collège des Bernardins, Paris, September 12, 2008

Without God, Mankind Loses Its Bearings

In our days, when in vast areas of the world the faith is in danger of dying out like a flame that no longer has fuel, the overriding priority is to make God present in this world and to show men and women the way to God. Not just any god, but the God who spoke on Sinai; to that God whose face we recognize in a love that presses "to the end" (cf. Jn 13:1)—in Jesus Christ, crucified and risen. The real problem at this moment of our history is that God is disappearing from the human horizon, and, with the dimming of the light that comes from God, mankind is losing its bearings, with increasingly evident destructive effects.

Letter to the Bishops of the Catholic Church, March 10, 2009

In Christ, God Has Loved Us to the Utmost

In the modern age, both faith and hope have undergone a "shift", because they have been relegated to the private and otherworldly sphere, while in day-to-day public life confidence in scientific and economic progress has been affirmed (cf. *Spe salvi*, no. 17). We all know that this progress is ambiguous: it opens up possibilities for good as well as evil. Technical developments and the improvement of social structures are important and certainly necessary, but they are not enough to guarantee the moral welfare of society (cf. ibid., no. 24). Man needs to be liberated from material oppressions, but more profoundly, he must be saved from the evils that afflict the spirit. And who can save him if not God, who is Love and has revealed his face as almighty and merciful Father in Jesus Christ? Our firm hope is therefore Christ: in him, God has loved us to the utmost and has given us life in abundance (cf. Jn 10:10), the life that every person, even if unknowingly, longs to possess.

Homily at the Holy Mass, Brno, Czech Republic, September 27, 2009

Creating Silence to Listen to God

We live in a society in which it seems that every space, every moment must be "filled" with projects, activities, and noise; there is often no time even to listen or to converse. Dear brothers and sisters, let us not fear to create silence, within and outside ourselves, if we wish to be able not only to become aware of God's voice but also to make out the voice of the person beside us, the voices of others.

Homily at the Holy Mass, Sulmona, Italy, July 4, 2010

God Is Concerned about Me

God personally looks after me, after us, after all mankind. I am not abandoned, adrift in the universe and in a society that leaves me ever more lost and bewildered. God looks after me. He is not a distant God, for whom my life is worthless.... It is fine and consoling to know that there is someone who loves me and looks after me. But it is far more important that there is a God who knows me, loves me, and is concerned about me. "I know my own and my own know me" (Jn 10:14), the Church says before the Gospel with the Lord's words. God knows me; he is concerned about me. This thought should make us truly joyful. Let us allow it to penetrate the depths of our being.

Homily at the Holy Mass at the Conclusion of the Year for Priests, June 11, 2010

God Serves Us and Gives Us Strength

We are God's servants; we are not his creditors but are always indebted to him, because we owe him everything since everything is a gift from him. Accepting and doing his will is the approach to have every day, at every moment of our life. Before God we must never present ourselves as if we believe we have done a service and deserve a great reward. This is an illusion that can be born in everyone, even in people who work very hard in the Lord's service, in the Church. Rather, we must be aware that in reality we never do enough for God. We must say, as Jesus suggests: "We are unworthy servants; we have only done what was our duty" (Lk 17:10). This is an attitude of humility that really puts us in our place and permits the Lord to be very generous to us. In fact, in another Gospel passage, he promises people that "he will put on his apron and have them sit at table, and he will come and serve them" (Lk 12:37). Dear friends, if we do God's will today with humility, without claiming anything from him, it will be Jesus himself who serves us, who helps us, who encourages us, who gives us strength and serenity.

Homily at the Holy Mass, Palermo, Italy, October 3, 2010

The Inexhaustible Imagination of God

[The Magi] were seeking traces of God; they were seeking to read his "signature" in creation; they knew that "the heavens are telling the glory of God" (Ps 19:1); they were certain, that is, that God can be perceived in creation. But, as sages, the Magi also knew that it is not with any kind of telescope but rather with the profound eyes of reason in search of the ultimate meaning of reality and with the desire for God, motivated by faith, that it is possible to meet him, indeed, becomes possible for God to come close to us. The universe is not the result of chance, as some would like to make us believe. In contemplating it, we are asked to interpret in it something profound: the wisdom of the Creator, the inexhaustible imagination of God, his infinite love for us. We must not let our minds be limited by theories that always go only so far and that—at a close look—are far from competing with faith but do not succeed in explaining the ultimate meaning of reality.

We cannot but perceive in the beauty of the world, its mystery, its greatness, and its rationality, the eternal rationality; nor can we dispense with its guidance to the one God, Creator of Heaven and of earth. If we acquire this perception, we shall see that the One who created the world and the One who was born in a grotto in

Bethlehem and who continues to dwell among us in the Eucharist is the same living God, who calls us, who loves us, and who wants to lead us to eternal life.

Homily at the Holy Mass for the Epiphany of the Lord, January 6, 2011

Christ, the One Supreme Law

At the center of the divine plan is Christ in whom God shows his face, in accord with the favor of his will. The Mystery hidden in the centuries is revealed in its fullness in the Word made flesh. And Paul then says: "In him all the fulness of God was pleased to dwell" (Col 1:19). In Christ the living God made himself close, visible, audible, and tangible so that each one might draw from his fullness of grace and truth (cf. Jn 1:14–16). Therefore, the whole of Christian life knows one supreme law, which Saint Paul expresses in a formula that recurs in all his holy writings: in Jesus Christ. Holiness, the fullness of Christian life, does not consist in carrying out extraordinary enterprises but in being united with Christ, in living his mysteries, in making our own his example, his thoughts, his behavior. The measure of holiness stems from the stature that Christ achieves in us, inasmuch as with the power of the Holy Spirit, we model our whole life on his. It is being conformed to Jesus, as Saint Paul says: "For those whom he foreknew he also predestined to be conformed to the image of his Son" (Rom 8:29). And Saint Augustine exclaimed: "My life shall be a real life, being wholly filled by you" (*Confessions*, bk. 10, no. 28). The Second Vatican Council, in the Dogmatic Constitution on the Church (*Lumen gentium*), speaks with clarity of the universal call to holiness, saying that no one is excluded: "The forms and tasks of life are many, but holiness is one—that sanctity which is cultivated by all who act under God's Spirit and ... follow Christ, poor, humble and cross-bearing, that they may deserve to be partakers of his glory" (*Lumen gentium*, no. 41).

General Audience, April 13, 2011

Losing Our Life in God, We Gain It

Each one of us must therefore ask himself: What place does God have in my life? Is he the Lord or am I? Overcoming the temptation to subject God to oneself and one's own interests, or to put him in a corner and be converted to the correct order of priorities, giving God first place, is a journey that each and every Christian must make over and over again. "Repent" is an invitation we shall often hear in Lent. It means following Jesus in such a way that his Gospel is a practical guide for life; it means letting God transform us, in order to stop thinking that we are the only ones to build our existence. It means recognizing that we are creatures, that we depend on God, on his love, and that only by "losing" our life in him can we gain it. This requires us to make our decisions in the light of the Word of God. Today it is no longer possible to be Christian as a mere consequence of living in a society that has Christian roots: even those who are born into a Christian family and receive a religious education must every day renew their decision to be Christian, that is, to give God first place in the face of the temptations that a secularized culture constantly suggests to them and in the face of the critical opinion of many of their contemporaries.

The trials to which society today subjects Christians are indeed numerous and affect their personal and social life. It is far from easy to be faithful to Christian marriage, to practice mercy in daily life, to make room for prayer and inner silence; it is far from easy to oppose publicly the decisions that many take for granted, such as abortion in the case of unwanted pregnancy, euthanasia in the case of serious illness, and embryo selection in order to prevent hereditary diseases. The temptation to set faith aside is always present, and conversion becomes a response to God that must be strengthened several times in life.... Our inner self must prepare to be visited by God and for this very reason must not let itself be invaded by illusions, appearances, and material things.

... Let us renew our commitment to the journey of conversion, to overcome the tendency to withdraw into ourselves and, instead, to make room for God, seeing daily reality with his eyes. The alternative between being closed into our own egotism and openness to the love of God and of others, we might say, corresponds to the alternative of the temptations of Jesus: an alternative, that is, between human power and love of the Cross, between redemption seen in material well-being alone and redemption as a work of God to which we should give primacy in life. Being converted means not shutting ourselves into the quest for our own success, our own prestige, our own status, but rather ensuring that every day, in the small things, truth, faith in God, and love become the most important things of all.

General Audience, February 13, 2013

To Believe Is to Touch the Hand of God in the Darkness of the World

"*Logos*" is not only a mathematical reason: "*Logos*" has a heart; "*Logos*" is also love. The truth is beautiful; truth and beauty go hand in hand: beauty is the seal of truth. Yet starting with the Psalms and with our everyday life, you have also strongly underlined that the "very good" of the sixth day—expressed by the Creator—is forever contradicted, in this world, by sin, by suffering, by corruption. And it almost seems that the devil wishes to soil creation permanently in order to contradict God and make his truth and his beauty irreconcilable. Also, in a world so marked by evil, the "*Logos*", eternal Beauty and eternal "*Ars*", must seem like the "*caput cruentatum*". The Incarnate Son, the Incarnate "*Logos*", is crowned with a crown of thorns; and yet in this way precisely, in this suffering figure of the Son of God, we begin to see the most profound beauty of our Creator and Redeemer. Even in the silence of the "darkness", listen to the Word. To believe is none other than, in the obscurity of the world, to touch the hand of God and thus, in silence, to hear the Word, to see Love.

Address at the Conclusion of the Spiritual Exercises for the Roman Curia, February 23, 2013

God's Yes Is Stronger
Than All of Us

Meditations on Faith

To Seek Christ: A Desire We Must Cultivate

Wherever God does not have pride of place, wherever he is not recognized and worshipped as the Supreme Good, human dignity is at risk. It is therefore urgent to bring our contemporaries to "rediscover" the authentic face of God, who revealed himself to us in Jesus Christ. Thus, the humanity of our time will also be able, like the Magi, to fall to their knees and adore him.

To seek Jesus must be the constant desire of believers, young people and adults, of the faithful, and of their pastors. This seeking must be encouraged, supported, and guided. Faith is not merely the attachment to a complex of dogmas, complete in itself, that is supposed to satisfy the thirst for God, present in the human heart. On the contrary, it guides man on his way through time toward a God who is ever new in his infinity. Christians, therefore, are at the same time both seekers and finders. It is precisely this that makes the Church young, open to the future, rich in hope for the whole of humanity.

Angelus, August 28, 2005

Believing Is Personal and Communitarian

Discovering the beauty and joy of faith is a path that every new generation must take on its own, for all that we have that is most our own and most intimate is staked on faith: our heart, our mind, our freedom, in a deeply personal relationship with the Lord at work within us. Just as radically, however, faith is a community act and attitude; it is the "we believe" of the Church. Thus, the joy of faith is a joy shared. Consequently, educating the new generations in the faith is an important and fundamental task that involves the entire Christian community.

Address at the Ecclesial Convention of the Diocese of Rome, June 5, 2006

Faith Can Be Reborn from the Wounds of History

We may all be tempted by the disbelief of Thomas. Suffering, evil, injustice, death—especially when it strikes the innocent, such as children who are victims of war and terrorism, of sickness and hunger—does not all of this put our faith to the test? Paradoxically, the disbelief of Thomas is most valuable to us in these cases, because it helps to purify all false concepts of God and leads us to discover his true face: the face of a God who, in Christ, has taken upon himself the wounds of injured humanity. Thomas has received from the Lord, and has in turn transmitted to the Church, the gift of a faith put to the test by the Passion and death of Jesus and confirmed by meeting him risen. His faith was almost dead but was born again thanks to his touching the wounds of Christ, those wounds that the Risen One did not hide but showed and continues to point out to us in the trials and sufferings of every human being.

How many wounds, how much suffering there is in the world! Natural calamities and human tragedies that cause innumerable victims and enormous material destruction are not lacking.... Through the wounds of the Risen Christ, we can see the evils that afflict humanity with the eyes of hope. In fact, by his rising, the Lord has not taken away suffering and evil from the world but has vanquished them at their roots by the super-abundance of his grace. He has countered the arrogance of evil with the supremacy of his love. He has left us the love that does not fear death, as the way to peace and joy. "Even as I have loved you"—he said to his disciples before his death—"that you also love one another" (cf. Jn 13:34).

"Urbi et Orbi" Message, April 8, 2007

The Commandments of God Are the Way to Freedom

Jesus reminded the rich young man that obedience to the Ten Commandments is necessary in order to "inherit eternal life". The Commandments are essential points of reference if we are to live in love, to distinguish clearly between good and evil, and to build a life plan that is solid and enduring.... Needless to say, these are questions that go against the grain in today's world, which advocates a freedom detached from values, rules, and objective norms and which encourages people to refuse to place limits on their immediate desires. But this is not the way to true freedom. It leads people to become enslaved to themselves, to their immediate desires, to idols like power, money, unbridled pleasure, and the entrapments of the world. It stifles their inborn vocation to love. God gives us the Commandments, because he wants to teach us true freedom. He wants to build a Kingdom of love, justice, and peace together with us. When we listen to the Commandments and put them into practice, it means not that we become estranged from ourselves but that we find the way to freedom and authentic love. The Commandments do not place limits on happiness but rather show us how to find it. At the beginning of the conversation with the rich young man, Jesus reminds him that the law that God gives is itself good, because "God is good."

Message for the Twenty-Fifth World Youth Day, February 22, 2010

Faith Makes Possible the Impossible

Jesus taught his disciples to grow in faith, to believe and to entrust themselves increasingly to him, in order to build their own lives on the rock. For this reason, they asked him, "Increase our faith!" (Lk 17:5). What they asked the Lord for is beautiful and is the fundamental request: disciples do not ask for material gifts, they do not ask for privileges, but they ask for the grace of faith, which guides and illumines the whole of life; they ask for the grace to recognize God and to be in a close relationship with him, receiving from him all his gifts, even those of courage, love, and hope.

Jesus, without directly answering their prayer, has recourse to a paradoxical image to express the incredible vitality of faith. Just as a lever raises something far heavier than its own weight, so faith, even a crumb of faith, can do unthinkable, extraordinary things, such as uproot a great tree and plant it in the sea (Lk 17:6). Faith trusting in Christ, welcoming him, letting him transform us, following him to the very end makes humanly impossible things possible in every situation.... The godless person, the one who does not behave in accordance with God, who trusts in his own power but is relying on a frail and inconsistent reality that will therefore give way, is destined to fall. The righteous person, on the other hand, trusts in a hidden but sound reality; he trusts in God and for this reason will have life.

Homily at the Holy Mass, Palermo, October 3, 2010

The Shattering Power of the Gospel

Faith gives you the power of God in order to be ever confident and courageous, to go ahead with new determination, to take the necessary initiatives to give your land an ever more beautiful face. And when you come up against the opposition of the world, may you hear the Apostle's words: "Do not be ashamed then of testifying to our Lord" (2 Tim 1:8). One should be ashamed of evil, of what offends God, of what offends man; one should be ashamed of the evil done to the Civil and Religious Community by actions that would prefer to remain in the shade! The temptation of discouragement and resignation comes to those who are weak in faith and those who confuse evil with good and to those who think that in the face of evil that is often profound there is nothing that can be done. On the contrary, those who are firmly founded on faith, who trust totally in God and who live in the Church, are capable of conveying the shattering power of the Gospel. This was how the saints who flourished in Palermo and throughout Sicily down the centuries behaved, as likewise the lay people and priests of today who are well known to you, such as, for example, Father Pino Puglisi. May they always keep you united and nourish in each one the desire to proclaim, with word and deed, the presence and love of Christ.

Homily at the Holy Mass, Palermo, October 3, 2010

Right Faith Directs Reason to Open Itself to God

Love desires to know better what it loves. Love, true love, does not make people blind but seeing. The thirst for knowledge, for a true knowledge of the other person, is part of love. For this reason, the Fathers of the Church found the precursors and forerunners of Christianity—outside the world of the revelation of Israel—not in the context of formal religion, but on the contrary in men in search of God, in search of the truth, in the "philosophers": in people who were thirsting for truth and were therefore on their way toward God. When this type of reason is not used, the great questions of humanity fall outside the context of reason and are left to irrationality. This is why an authentic theology is so important. Right faith directs reason to open itself to the divine, so that, guided by love for the truth, it may know God more closely. The initiative for this journey is with God, who has placed in human hearts the desire to seek his face.

Address at the Conferral of the Ratzinger Prize, June 30, 2011

Faith: Joining Ourselves Personally to God's Self-Revelation

Certainly, there are many people today who feel attracted by the figure of Christ and want to know him better. They realize that he is the answer to so many of our deepest concerns. But who is he really? How can someone who lived on this earth so long ago have anything in common with me today? ... Faith is more than just empirical or historical facts; it is an ability to grasp the mystery of Christ's Person in all its depth.

Yet faith is not the result of human effort, of human reasoning, but rather a gift of God: "Blessed are you, Simon Bar-Jona! For flesh and blood has not revealed this to you, but my Father who is in heaven" (Mt 16:17). Faith starts with God, who opens his heart to us and invites us to share in his own divine life. Faith does not simply provide information about who Christ is; rather, it entails a personal relationship with Christ, a joining of our whole person, with all our understanding, will, and feelings, to God's self-revelation. So Jesus' question "But who do you say that I am?" (Mk 8:29) is ultimately a challenge to the disciples to make a personal decision in his regard. Faith in Christ and discipleship are strictly interconnected. And, since faith involves following the Master, it must become constantly stronger, deeper, and more mature, to the extent that it leads to a closer and more intense relationship with Jesus. Peter and the other disciples also had to grow in this way, until their encounter with the Risen Lord opened their eyes to the fullness of faith.

Homily at the Holy Mass, World Youth Day, Madrid, August 21, 2011

God Enters Our Lives to Free Us

Though often marked by sorrows, uncertainties, and moments of crisis, our history is a history of salvation and of a "restoration of fortunes" (see Ps 126:1). In Jesus, every exile comes to an end, and every tear is dried, in the mystery of the Cross, of death transformed into life, like the grain of wheat that breaks in the earth and sprouts.

For us, too, this discovery of Jesus Christ is the great joy of God's Yes, of the restoration of our fortunes. Those who returned from Babylon full of joy found a poor, devastated homeland—like the difficult time of sowing described in Psalm 126—and they suffered and wept in the uncertainty of whether there would really be a harvest. Like them, we, too, after the great discovery of Jesus Christ—our life, the truth, the way—often enter the terrain of faith, the "land of faith", only to find that life is hard, dark, and difficult, a sowing in tears. But we are sure that in the end, the light of Christ will really give us that great harvest. We must learn this also in the dark nights; do not forget that the light is there, that God is already in our lives, and that we can sow with the great trust that God's Yes is stronger than all of us.

This meditation translated by Thomas Jacobi, Ignatius Press.

It is important not to lose this memory of God's presence in our lives, this profound joy that God has entered our lives and freed us. It is gratitude for the discovery of Jesus Christ, who has come into our midst. And this gratitude transforms into hope. It is the star of hope that gives us trust. It is light, because the pains of sowing are the beginning of new life, of the great, definitive joy of God.

General Audience, October 12, 2011

Faith Brings Us into the Restlessness of God

Man has an innate restlessness for God, but this restlessness is a participation in God's own restlessness for us. Since God is concerned about us, he follows us even into the manger, even to the Cross.... For faith is nothing less than being interiorly seized by God, something that guides us along the pathways of life. Faith draws us into a state of being seized by the restlessness of God, and it makes us pilgrims who are on an inner journey toward the true King of the world and his promise of justice, truth, and love.

Faith's inner pilgrimage toward God occurs above all in prayer. Saint Augustine once said that prayer is ultimately nothing more than the realization and radicalization of our yearning for God. Instead of "yearning", we could also translate the word as "restlessness" and say that prayer would detach us from our false security, from our being enclosed within material and visible realities, and would give us a restlessness for God and thus an openness to and concern for one another.

Homily at the Holy Mass, Epiphany of the Lord, January 6, 2013

Believing Means Letting God Enter
Our Lives Every Day

The event of the Incarnation, of God who became man, like us, shows us the daring realism of divine love. God's action, in fact, was not limited to words. On the contrary, we might say that he was not content with speaking, but entered into our history, taking upon himself the effort and burden of human life. The Son of God truly became a man. He was born of the Virgin Mary in a specific time and place, in Bethlehem during the reign of the Emperor Augustus, under the Governor Quirinius (cf. Lk 2:1–2); he grew up in a family, he had friends, he formed a group of disciples, he instructed the Apostles to continue his mission, and he ended the course of his earthly life on the Cross. The way God acted gives us a strong incentive to question ourselves on the reality of our faith, which must not be limited to the sphere of sentiment, of the emotions; rather, it must enter into the practicality of our existence, that is, it must touch our everyday life and give it practical guidance. God did not stop at words, but showed us how to live, sharing in our own experience, except for sin.... Faith has a fundamental aspect that involves not only our mind and heart but also our whole life.

General Audience, January 9, 2013

The Journey of Faith Opens to Life

Saying "I believe in God" means founding my life on him, letting his Word guide it every day, in practical decisions, without fear of losing some part of myself.... Faith makes us pilgrims on earth, integrated into the world and into history, but bound for the Heavenly Homeland. Believing in God thus makes us harbingers of values that often do not coincide with the fashion and opinion of the moment. It requires us to adopt criteria and assume forms of conduct that are not part of the common mindset. Christians must not be afraid to go "against the current" in order to live their faith, resisting the temptation to "conform". In many of our societies, God has become the "great absent One", and many idols have supplanted him, multiform idols, especially possession and the autonomous "I". And even the major and positive breakthroughs of science and technology have instilled in people an illusion of omnipotence and self-sufficiency and an increasing egotism that has created many imbalances in interpersonal relations and social behavior.

Nevertheless, the thirst for God (cf. Ps 63:1–2) has not been quenched, and the Gospel message continues to resonate in the words and deeds of numerous men and women of faith. Abraham, the father of believers, continues to be a father of many children who agree to walk in his footsteps and set out in obedience to the divine call, trusting in the benevolent presence of the Lord and receiving his blessing in order to become themselves a blessing for all. It is the blessed world of faith to which we are all called, in order to walk fearlessly, following the Lord Jesus Christ. And at times it is a difficult journey that also undergoes trial and death but that opens to life in a radical transformation of reality that only the eyes of faith can perceive and enjoy to the full.

Affirming "I believe in God" impels us, therefore, to set out, to come out of ourselves, exactly as Abraham did, to bring to the daily situation in which we live the certainty that comes to us from faith: namely, the certainty of God's presence in history today too; a presence that brings life and salvation and opens us to a future with him for a fullness of life that will know no end.

General Audience, January 23, 2013

In Temptation, God Is at Stake

The tempter is cunning. He does not directly impel us toward evil but rather impels us toward a false good, making us believe that the true realities are power and everything that satisfies our primary needs. In this way, God becomes secondary; he is reduced to a means. In short, he becomes unreal, he no longer counts, he disappears. Ultimately, in temptation faith is at stake, because God is at stake. Not only at the crucial moments in life but also, when one looks closer, at every moment, we stand at a crossroads: Do we want to follow our own ego or God? Our individual interests or the true Good, to follow what is *really* good?

As the Fathers of the Church teach us, the temptations are part of Jesus' "descent" into our human condition, into the abyss of sin and its consequences; a "descent" that Jesus made to the end, even to death on the Cross and to the hell of extreme remoteness from God. In this way, he is the hand that God stretches out to man, to the lost sheep, to bring him back to safety. As Saint Augustine teaches, Jesus took the temptations from us to give us his victory (cf. *Enarrationes in Psalmos*, 60, 3 [*PL* 36, 724]). Therefore, let us not be afraid either of facing the battle against the spirit of evil: the important thing is to fight it with him, with Christ, the Victor.

Angelus, February 17, 2013

The Love That Comes from God Is Eternal

Meditations on Love

Only Love Can Save Us

Only from the saints, only from God does true revolution come, the definitive way to change the world. In the last century, we experienced revolutions with a common program—expecting nothing more from God, they assumed total responsibility for the cause of the world in order to change it. And this, as we saw, meant that a human and partial point of view was always taken as an absolute guiding principle. Absolutizing what is not absolute but relative is called totalitarianism. It does not liberate man but takes away his dignity and enslaves him. It is not ideologies that save the world, but only a return to the living God, our Creator, the guarantor of our freedom, the guarantor of what is really good and true. True revolution consists in simply turning to God, who is the measure of what is right and who at the same time is everlasting love. And what could ever save us apart from love?

Address at World Youth Day Vigil, Cologne, August 20, 2005

Love Comes from God

Love of God and love of neighbor are ... inseparable; they form a single commandment. But both live from the love of God, who has loved us first. No longer is it a question, then, of a "commandment" imposed from without and calling for the impossible, but rather it is a question of a freely bestowed experience of love from within, a love that by its very nature must then be shared with others. Love grows through love. Love is "divine", because it comes from God and unites us to God; through this unifying process, it makes us a "we" that transcends our divisions and makes us one, until in the end God is "everything to every one" (1 Cor 15:28).

Encyclical Letter Deus caritas est, *December 25, 2005*

Faith Gives Rise to Love

Faith, hope, and charity go together. Hope is practiced through the virtue of patience, which continues to do good even in the face of apparent failure, and through the virtue of humility, which accepts God's mystery and trusts him even in times of darkness. Faith tells us that God has given his Son for our sakes and gives us the victorious certainty that it is really true: God is love! It thus transforms our impatience and our doubts into the sure hope that God holds the world in his hands and that, as the dramatic imagery at the end of the Book of Revelation points out, in spite of all darkness he ultimately triumphs in glory. Faith, which sees the love of God revealed in the pierced heart of Jesus on the Cross, gives rise to love. Love is the light—and in the end, the only light—that can always illuminate a world grown dim and give us the courage needed to keep living and working. Love is possible, and we are able to practice it, because we are created in the image of God.

Encyclical Letter Deus caritas est, *December 25, 2005*

For Love, God Becomes Our Slave

God loves his creature, man; he even loves him in his fall and does not leave him to himself. He loves him to the end. He is impelled with his love to the very end, to the extreme: he came down from his divine glory. He cast aside the raiment of his divine glory and put on the garb of a slave. He came down to the extreme lowliness of our fall. He kneels before us and carries out for us the service of a slave: he washes our dirty feet so that we might be admitted to God's banquet and be made worthy to take our place at his table—something that on our own we neither could nor would ever be able to do.

God is not a remote God, too distant or too great to be bothered with our trifles. Since God is great, he can also be concerned with small things. Since he is great, the soul of man, the same man, created through eternal love, is not a small thing but great and worthy of God's love. God's holiness is not merely an incandescent power before which we are obliged to withdraw, terrified. It is a power of love and therefore a purifying and healing power.

God descends and becomes a slave; he washes our feet so that we may come to his table. In this, the entire mystery of Jesus Christ is expressed. In this, what redemption means becomes visible. The basin in which he washes us is his love, ready to face death. Only love has that purifying power, which washes the grime from us and elevates us to God's heights. The basin that purifies us is God himself, who gives himself to us without reserve—to the very depths of his suffering and his death. He is ceaselessly this love that cleanses us; in the sacraments of purification—Baptism and the Sacrament of Penance—he is continually on his knees at our feet and carries out for us the service of a slave, the service of purification, making us capable of God. His love is inexhaustible; it truly goes to the very end.

Homily at the Holy Mass, Holy Thursday, April 13, 2006

God Is an Event of Love

In the course of human history, a thick layer of dirt has covered God's good creation, which makes it difficult if not impossible to perceive in it the Creator's reflection, although the knowledge of the Creator's existence is reawakened within us ever anew, as it were, spontaneously, at the sight of a sunset over the sea, on an excursion to the mountains, or before a flower that has just bloomed.

But the Creator Spirit comes to our aid. He has entered history and speaks to us in a new way. In Jesus Christ, God himself was made man and allowed us, so to speak, to cast a glance at the intimacy of God himself. And there we see something totally unexpected: in God, an "I" and a "You" exist. The mysterious God is not infinite loneliness; he is an event of love. If by gazing at creation we think we can glimpse the Creator Spirit, God himself, rather like creative mathematics, like a force that shapes the laws of the world and their order, but then, even, also like beauty, now we come to realize: the Creator Spirit has a heart. He is Love. The Son who speaks to the Father exists, and they are both one in the Spirit, who constitutes, so to speak, the atmosphere of giving and loving that makes them one God. This unity of love that is God is a unity far more sublime than the unity of a last indivisible particle could be. The Triune God himself is the one and only God.

Homily at the Holy Mass, Pentecost, Meeting with the Ecclesial Movements and New Communities, June 3, 2006

It Is the Spirit Who Makes Us Love

The newness of Jesus consists essentially in the fact that he himself "fulfills" the Commandments with the love of God, with the power of the Holy Spirit, who dwells within him. And we, through faith in Christ, can open ourselves to the action of the Holy Spirit, who makes us capable of living divine love. So it is that every precept becomes true as a requirement of love, and all join in a single commandment: love God with all your heart and love your neighbor as yourself.

Angelus, February 13, 2011

Whoever Loves Is Capable of a New Beginning

How can we imitate Jesus? He said: "Love your enemies and pray for those who persecute you, so that you may be sons of your Father who is in heaven" (Mt 5:44–45). Anyone who welcomes the Lord into his life and loves him with all his heart is capable of a new beginning. He succeeds in doing God's will: to bring about a new form of existence enlivened by love and destined for eternity. The Apostle Paul added: "Do you not know that you are God's temple and that God's Spirit dwells in you?" (1 Cor 3:16). If we are truly aware of this reality and our life is profoundly shaped by it, then our witness becomes clear, eloquent, and effective.

Angelus, February 20, 2011

Praying Is Human, Because God Is Human

Meditations on Prayer

In Prayer, We Open Ourselves to Others

Prayer is a crucible in which our expectations and aspirations are exposed to the light of God's Word, immersed in dialogue with the One who is the Truth, and from which they emerge free from hidden lies and compromises with various forms of selfishness (cf. *Spe salvi*, no. 33). Without the dimension of prayer, the human "I" ends by withdrawing into himself, and the conscience, which should be an echo of God's voice, risks being reduced to a mirror of the self, so that the inner conversation becomes a monologue, giving rise to self-justifications by the thousands.

Therefore, prayer is a guarantee of openness to others: whoever frees himself for God and his needs simultaneously opens himself to the other, to the brother or sister who knocks at the door of his heart and asks to be heard, asks for attention, forgiveness, at times correction, but always in fraternal charity. True prayer is never self-centered; it is always centered on the other. As such, it opens the person praying to the "ecstasy" of charity, to the capacity to go out of oneself to draw close to the other in humble, neighborly service. True prayer is the driving force of the world since it keeps it open to God. For this reason, without prayer there is no hope, but only illusion. In fact, it is not God's presence that alienates man but his absence: without the true God, Father of the Lord Jesus Christ, illusory hopes become an invitation to escape from reality. Speaking with God, dwelling in his presence, letting oneself be illuminated and purified by his Word introduces us, instead, into the heart of reality, into the very motor of becoming cosmic; it introduces us, so to speak, to the beating heart of the universe.

Homily at the Holy Mass, Ash Wednesday, February 6, 2008

Prayer Is Receptivity to God's Grace

The grace of the Spirit ... is something we cannot merit or achieve, but only receive as pure gift. God's love can unleash its power only when it is allowed to change us from within. We have to let it break through the hard crust of our indifference, our spiritual weariness, our blind conformity to the spirit of this age. Only then can we let it ignite our imagination and shape our deepest desires. That is why prayer is so important: daily prayer, private prayer in the quiet of our hearts and before the Blessed Sacrament, and liturgical prayer in the heart of the Church. Prayer is pure receptivity to God's grace, love in action, communion with the Spirit, who dwells within us, leading us, through Jesus in the Church, to our heavenly Father. In the power of his Spirit, Jesus is always present in our hearts, quietly waiting for us to be still with him, to hear his voice, to abide in his love, and to receive "power from on high", enabling us to be salt and light for our world.

Homily at the Holy Mass, World Youth Day, Sydney, July 20, 2008

Prayer Is Like a Stairway

From God we do not ask something small or great; from God we invoke the divine gift, God himself; this is the great gift that God gives us: God himself. In this regard, we must learn to pray, to pray for the great reality, for the divine reality, so that God may give us himself, may give us his Spirit and thus we may respond to the demands of life and help others in their suffering.

Of course, the Our Father teaches us this. We can pray for many things. In all our needs, we can pray: "Help me!" This is very human, and God is human, as we have seen; therefore, it is right to pray to God also for the small things of our daily lives.

However, at the same time, prayer is a journey, I would say a stairway: we must learn more and more what it is that we can pray for and what we cannot pray for because it is an expression of our selfishness. I cannot pray for things that are harmful for others; I cannot pray for things that help my egoism, my pride. Thus prayer, in God's eyes, becomes a process of purification of our thoughts, of our desires. As the Lord says in the Parable of the Vine: we must be pruned, purified, every day; living with Christ, in Christ, abiding in Christ is a process of purification, and it is only in this process of slow purification, of liberation from ourselves and from the desire to have only ourselves, that the true journey of life lies and the path of joy unfolds.

Address to the Seminarians of the Pontifical Roman Major Seminary, February 12, 2010

"In" the World through Prayer

True prayer is not at all foreign to reality. If prayer should alienate you, remove you from your real life, be on your guard: it would not be true prayer! On the contrary, dialogue with God is a guarantee of truth, of truth with ourselves and with others and hence of freedom. Being with God, listening to his word, in the Gospel and in the Church's Liturgy, protects you from the dazzle of pride and presumption, from fashions and conformism, and gives you the strength to be truly free, even from certain temptations masked by good things. You asked me: How can we be "in" the world but not "of" the world? I answer you: precisely through prayer, through personal contact with God. It is not a question of multiplying words—Jesus already said this to us— but of being in God's presence, of making our own, in our minds and in our hearts, the words of the Our Father that embraces all the problems of our lives, or by adoring the Eucharist, meditating on the Gospel in our room, or participating with recollection in the Liturgy. None of this removes us from life but instead helps us truly to be ourselves in every context, faithful to the voice of God, who speaks to our conscience, free from the conditioning of the time!

Meeting with Young People, Sulmona, Italy, July 4, 2010

Man in Every Age Prays

Man has prayed in every age, because he cannot fail to wonder about the meaning of his life, which remains obscure and discomforting if it is not put in relation to the mystery of God and of his plan for the world.

Human life is a fabric woven of good and of evil, of undeserved suffering and of joy and beauty that spontaneously and irresistibly impel us to ask God for that light and that inner strength that support us on earth and reveal a hope beyond the boundaries of death.

General Audience, May 4, 2011

Prayer: An Expression of the Desire for God

We live in an age in which the signs of secularism are glaringly obvious. God seems to have disappeared from the horizon of some people or to have become a reality that meets with indifference. Yet at the same time we see many signs of a reawakening of the religious sense, a rediscovery of the importance of God to the human being's life, a need for spirituality, for going beyond a purely horizontal and materialistic vision of human life.... Man bears within him a thirst for the infinite, a longing for eternity, a quest for beauty, a desire for love, a need for light and for truth that impel him toward the Absolute; man bears within him the desire for God. And man knows, in a certain way, that he can turn to God; he knows he can pray to him. Saint Thomas Aquinas, one of the greatest theologians in history, defines prayer as "an expression of man's desire for God".

This attraction to God, which God himself has placed in man, is the soul of prayer, that then takes on a great many forms, in accordance with the history, the time, the moment, the grace, and even the sin of every person praying. Man's history has in fact known various forms of prayer, because he has developed different kinds of openness to the "Other" and to the Beyond, so that we may recognize prayer as an experience present in every religion and culture.

Prayer is centered and rooted in the inmost depths of the person; it is therefore not easily decipherable and, for the same reason, can be subject to misunderstanding and mystification. In this sense, too, we can understand the expression: prayer is difficult. In fact, prayer is the place par excellence of free giving, of striving for the Invisible, the Unexpected, and the Ineffable.

Therefore, the experience of prayer is a challenge to everyone, a "grace" to invoke, a gift of the One to whom we turn.

General Audience, May 11, 2011

In Prayer, We See the Fire of God

Whenever God disappears, man falls into the slavery of idolatry, as the totalitarian regimes demonstrated in our time and as the various forms of nihilism that make man dependent on idols, on idolatry, also demonstrate; they enslave him.

Secondly, the primary aim of prayer is conversion, the flame of God that transforms our hearts and enables us to see God and so to live in accordance with God and live for others. And the third point: The Fathers tell us that this history of a prophet is prophetic too, if, they say, it foreshadows the future, the future Christ; it is a step on the journey toward Christ. And they tell us that here we see God's true fire: the love that guided the Lord even to the Cross, to the total gift of himself. True worship of God, therefore, is giving oneself to God and to men and women; true worship is love. And true worship of God does not destroy but renews, transforms.

Of course, the fire of God, the fire of love, burns, transforms, purifies but in this very way does not destroy but rather creates the truth of our being, recreates our hearts. And thus, truly alive through the grace of the fire of the Holy Spirit, of love of God, we are worshippers in spirit and in truth.

General Audience, June 15, 2011

We Are Certain of God's Presence

Beset by many problems, we are tempted to think that perhaps God does not save me, that he does not know me, perhaps he is not able to; the temptation to lose faith is our enemy's ultimate attack, and if we are to find God, if we are to find life, we must resist it....

The human being cries out in anguish, in danger, in pain; the human being calls for help, and God answers. In this interweaving of the human cry and the divine response, we find the dialectic of prayer and the key to reading the entire history of salvation. The cry expresses the need for help and appeals to the other's faithfulness; crying out means making an act of faith in God's closeness and in his willingness to listen. Prayer expresses the certainty of a divine presence already experienced and believed in that is fully expressed in God's salvific answers. This is important: that in our prayer the certainty of God's presence be given importance and be made present.

General Audience, September 7, 2011

We Are Made for Eternity

Meditations for Young People and Families

Growing in the Certainty of Being Loved by the Lord

The source of Christian joy is the certainty of being loved by God, loved personally by our Creator, by the One who holds the entire universe in his hands and loves each one of us and the whole great human family with a passionate and faithful love, a love greater than our infidelities and sins, a love that forgives. This love "is so great that it turns God against himself", as appears definitively in the mystery of the Cross: "So great is God's love for man that by becoming man he follows him even into death, and so reconciles justice and love" (*Deus caritas est*, no. 10).

... In other words: Jesus said he was the "Way" that leads to the Father, as well as the "Truth" and the "Life" (cf. Jn 14:5–7). Thus, the question is, How can our children and young people, practically and existentially, find in him this path of salvation and joy? This is precisely the great mission for which the Church—as the family of God and the company of friends into which we are already integrated with Baptism as tiny children—exists and in which our faith and joy and the certainty of being loved by the Lord must grow. It is therefore indispensable ... that the new generations experience the Church as a company of friends who are truly dependable and close in all life's moments and circumstances, whether joyful and gratifying or arduous and obscure; as a company that will never fail us, not even in death, for it carries within it the promise of eternity.

Address at the Ecclesial Convention of the Diocese of Rome, June 5, 2006

The Family Is a Necessary Good for Society

The family is an intermediate institution between individuals and society, and nothing can completely take its place. The family is itself based primarily on a deep interpersonal relationship between husband and wife, sustained by affection and mutual understanding. To enable this, it receives abundant help from God in the Sacrament of Matrimony, which brings with it a true vocation to holiness. Would that our children might experience more the harmony and affection between their parents, rather than disagreements and discord, since the love between father and mother is a source of great security for children and teaches them the beauty of a faithful and lasting love.

The family is a necessary good for peoples, an indispensable foundation for society, and a great and lifelong treasure for couples. It is a unique good for children, who are meant to be the fruit of the love, of the total and generous self-giving of their parents. To proclaim the whole truth about the family, based on marriage as *a domestic Church and a sanctuary of life*, is a great responsibility incumbent upon all.

Address at the Fifth World Meeting of Families Prayer Vigil, Valencia, Spain, July 8, 2006

God Gives Young People a Beautiful Life

Wondering about the definitive future awaiting each of us gives full meaning to our existence. It directs our life plan toward horizons that are not limited and fleeting, but broad and deep, and that motivate us to love this world that God loves so deeply, to devote ourselves to its development with the freedom and joy born of faith and hope. Against these horizons we do not see earthly reality as absolute, and we sense that God is preparing a greater future for us. In this way, we can say with Saint Augustine: "Let us long for our home on high, let us pine for our home in heaven, let us feel that we are strangers here" (*Tractates on the Gospel of Saint John*, 35.9). With his gaze fixed on eternal life, Blessed Pier Giorgio Frassati, who died in 1925 at the age of twenty-four, could say: "I want to live, not just mess around!" On a photograph taken while mountain climbing, he wrote to a friend: "To the heights", referring not only to Christian perfection but also to eternal life.

Dear young friends, I urge you to keep this perspective in developing your life plan: we are called to eternity. God created us to be with him, forever. This will help you to make meaningful decisions and live a beautiful life.

Message for the Twenty-Fifth World Youth Day, March 28, 2010

Young People Thirst for the Future

The thirst that young people carry in their hearts is a desire for meaning and authentic human relationships that will help them not to feel alone before the challenges of life. It is a desire for a future rendered less uncertain by a sure and trustworthy companionship that stands at the side of each person with delicacy and respect, offering strong values from which to set out toward goals that are high, but not impossible to achieve. Our answer is the proclamation of God, the friend of man, who through Jesus became close to each one of us. The transmission of the faith is an inalienable part of the integral formation of the person, because in Jesus Christ the hope of a fulfilled life is realized: as the Second Vatican Council teaches, "Whoever follows Christ the perfect man becomes himself more a man" (*Gaudium et spes*, no. 41). The personal encounter with Jesus is the key to understanding the importance of God in our daily existence, the secret of how to live it in brotherly love, the condition that makes it possible to pick ourselves up after a fall and to move toward constant conversion.

Address to the Bishops at the Sixty-First General Assembly of the Italian Episcopal Conference, May 27, 2010

The Meaning of Life Sprouts in the Family

The relationship between parents and children, as you know, is fundamental but not only due to a rightful tradition. It is something more, which Jesus himself taught us: it is the torch of faith that is passed on from one generation to the next; that flame which is also present in the Rite of Baptism, when the priest says: "Receive the light of Christ.... This light is entrusted to you to be kept burning brightly."

The family is fundamental, because that is where the first awareness of the meaning of life germinates in the human soul. It germinates in the relationship with the mother and with the father, who are not the masters of their children's lives but are God's primary collaborators in the transmission of life and faith....

The image of a tree is very significant for representing the human person.... The image of the tree tells us that each one of us needs fertile ground in which to sink our own roots, a ground rich with nutritious substances that make a person grow: these are values, but above all they are love and faith, the knowledge of God's true face, the awareness that he loves us infinitely, faithfully, patiently, to the point of giving his life for us. In this sense, the family is a "Church in miniature", because it transmits God, transmits Christ's love, by virtue of the Sacrament of Matrimony. Divine love, which unites a man and a woman and makes them become parents, is capable of generating in the hearts of their children the seed of faith, that is, the light of the deep meaning of life.... The family, to be this "Church in miniature", must be properly inserted in the "great Church", that is, in the family of God that Christ came to form.... Together with the family one is born into, the great family of the Church is fundamental, encountered and experienced in the parish community and in the diocese.... Indeed, even ecclesial movements and associations serve not themselves but Christ and the Church.

Address to the Young People of Sicily, Salerno, October 3, 2010

The Important Witness of Christian Families

Everyone knows that the Christian family is a special sign
of the presence and love of Christ and that it is called to
give a specific and irreplaceable contribution to evangelization.... The Christian family has always been the
first way of transmitting the faith and still today retains
great possibilities for evangelization in many areas.

By the grace of God, many Christian families today
are acquiring an ever deeper awareness of their mission-
ary vocation and are devoting themselves seriously to
bearing witness to Christ the Lord.... In today's society, the presence of exemplary Christian families is more
necessary and urgent than ever. Unfortunately, we are
forced to acknowledge the spread of a secularization that
leads to the exclusion of God from life and the increasing disintegration of the family, especially in Europe.
Freedom without commitment to the truth is made
into an absolute, and individual well-being through the
consumption of material goods and transient experiences is cultivated as an ideal, obscuring the quality of
interpersonal relations and deeper human values; love
is reduced to sentimental emotion and to the gratifica-
tion of instinctive impulses, without a commitment to
build lasting bonds of reciprocal belonging and without openness to life. We are called to oppose such a

mentality! Alongside what the Church says, the testimony and commitment of the Christian family—your concrete testimony—is very important, especially when you affirm the inviolability of human life from conception until natural death, the singular and irreplaceable value of the family founded upon matrimony, and the need for legislation that supports families in the task of giving birth to children and educating them.

Homily at the Holy Mass, National Day of Croatian Catholic Families, Zagabria, June 5, 2011

In Marriage, the Spouses Give Their Very Lives

We are called to receive and to pass on the truths of faith in a spirit of harmony, to live our love for each other and for everyone, sharing joys and sufferings, learning to seek and to grant forgiveness, valuing the different charisms under the leadership of the bishops. In a word, we have been given the task of building church communities that are more and more like families, able to reflect the beauty of the Trinity and to evangelize not only by word, but I would say by "radiation", in the strength of living love.

It is not only the Church that is called to be the image of One God in Three Persons, but also the family, based on marriage between man and woman.... God created us male and female, equal in dignity, but also with respective and complementary characteristics, so that the two might be a gift for each other, might value each other, and might bring into being a community of love and life. It is love that makes the human person the authentic image of the Blessed Trinity, image of God....

Dear married couples, in living out your marriage, you are giving each other not any particular thing or activity but your whole lives. And your love is fruitful first and foremost for yourselves, because you desire and accomplish one another's good and you experience the joy of receiving and giving.

It is also fruitful in your generous and responsible procreation of children, in your attentive care for them, and in their vigilant and wise education. And lastly, it is fruitful for society, because family life is the first and irreplaceable school of social virtues, such as respect for persons, gratuitousness, trust, responsibility, solidarity, cooperation.

Dear married couples, watch over your children and, in a world dominated by technology, transmit to them, with serenity and trust, the reasons for living, the strength of faith, pointing them toward high goals and supporting them in their fragility.

And let me add a word to the children here: be sure that you always maintain a relationship of deep affection and attentive care for your parents, and see that your relationships with your brothers and sisters are opportunities to grow in love.

Homily at the Holy Mass, Milan, Italy, June 3, 2012

Families Open to Others, Attentive to the Poor, Responsible in Society

The vocation to love is a wonderful thing. It is the only force that can truly transform the cosmos, the world. You have before you the witness of so many families who point out the paths for growing in love: by maintaining a constant relationship with God and participating in the life of the Church, by cultivating dialogue, by respecting the other's point of view, by being ready for service and patient with the failings of others, by being able to forgive and to seek forgiveness, by overcoming with intelligence and humility any conflicts that may arise, by agreeing on principles of upbringing, and by being open to other families, attentive toward the poor, and responsible within civil society.

These are all elements that build up the family. Live them with courage, and be sure that, insofar as you live your love for each other and for all with the help of God's grace, you become a living Gospel, a true domestic Church (cf. *Familiaris consortio*, no. 49).

Homily at the Holy Mass, Milan, Italy, June 3, 2012

A Utilitarian Mentality Does Not Lead
to Harmonious Development

In modern economic theories, there is often a utilitarian concept of work, production, and the market. Yet God's plan, as well as experience, shows that the one-sided logic of sheer utility and maximum profit is not conducive to harmonious development, to the good of the family, or to building a just society, because it brings in its wake ferocious competition, strong inequalities, degradation of the environment, the race for consumer goods, family tensions. Indeed, the utilitarian mentality tends to take its toll on personal and family relationships, reducing them to a fragile convergence of individual interests and undermining the solidity of the social fabric.

Homily at the Holy Mass, Milan, Italy, June 3, 2012

Trust Joyfully in God's Promises

Meditations on Hope

Called to Be Apostles of Hope

Confronted by today's changing and complex panorama, the virtue of hope is subject to harsh trials in the community of believers. For this very reason, we must be apostles who are filled with hope and joyful trust in God's promises. God never abandons his people; indeed, he invites them to conversion so that his Kingdom may become a reality. The Kingdom of God means not only that God exists, that he is alive, but also that he is present and active in the world. He is the most intimate and crucial reality in every act of human life, every moment of history.

Address to the Mexican Bishops, September 23, 2005

No Shadow Can Obscure Christ's Light

In the earthly Jesus, the culmination of creation and of history is found, but in the Risen Christ, this is surpassed: the passage through death to eternal life anticipates the point of the "recapitulation" of all things in Christ (cf. Eph 1:10). Indeed "all things", the Apostle wrote, "were created through him and for him" (Col 1:16). And it is precisely with the resurrection of the dead that he became "in everything ... pre-eminent" (Col 1:18). Jesus himself affirms this, appearing to his disciples after the Resurrection: "All authority in heaven and on earth has been given to me" (Mt 28:18). This awareness supports the way of the Church, Body of Christ, on the paths of history. There is no shadow, however dark, that can obscure Christ's light. This is why believers in Christ never lack hope, even today, in the face of the great social and financial crisis that is tormenting humanity, in the face of the destructive hatred and violence that have not ceased to stain many of the earth's regions with blood, in the face of the selfishness and pretension of the human being in establishing himself as his own God, which sometimes leads to dangerous distortions of the divine plan concerning life and the dignity of the human being, the family, and the harmony of the creation. Our efforts to free human life and the world from the forms of poison and contamination that could destroy the present and the future retain their value and meaning ..., because "it is the great hope based upon God's promises that gives us courage and directs our action in good times and bad" (*Spe salvi*, no. 35).

Homily at the Holy Mass, Epiphany of the Lord, January 6, 2009

God Alone Is Our Firm Hope

It is impossible to live without hope. Experience shows that all things, even our life, are at risk; they can collapse for some internal or external reason at any moment. It is normal: all that is human, hence therefore also hope, has no basis in itself but needs a "rock" to which to be anchored. This is why Paul writes that Christians are called to base human hope on the "Living God". In him alone does it become safe and dependable. Actually, only God, who revealed the fullness of his love to us in Jesus Christ, can be our firm hope. Indeed, in him, our hope, we have been saved (cf. Rom 8:24).

However, be careful: in times like these, given the cultural and social context in which we are living, there may be a greater risk of reducing Christian hope to an ideology, to a group slogan, or to outward appearances. Nothing is more contrary to Jesus' message! He does not want his disciples to "recite" a part, even that of hope. He wants them "to be" hope, and they can be hope only if they remain united to him!

Homily at the Holy Mass, Fourth Anniversary of the Death of John Paul II, April 2, 2009

His Resurrection: A Bridge between the World and Eternal Life

The Resurrection of the Lord assures us that the divine plan of salvation, despite all the obscurity of history, will certainly be brought about. This is why his Passover truly is our hope. And we, risen with Christ through Baptism, must now follow him faithfully in holiness of life, advancing towards the eternal Passover, sustained by the knowledge that the difficulties, struggles and trials of human life, including death, henceforth can no longer separate us from Him and his love. His Resurrection has formed a bridge between the world and eternal life over which every man and every woman can cross to reach the true goal of our earthly pilgrimage.

Regina Caeli, April 13, 2009

Those Who Suffer Wait for the Hope of the Risen One

Today, even in this modern age marked by anxiety and uncertainty, we relive the event of the Resurrection, which changed the face of our life and changed the history of humanity. From the Risen Christ, all those who are still oppressed by chains of suffering and death look for hope, sometimes even without knowing it.

May the Risen Lord grant that the strength of his life, peace, and freedom be experienced everywhere. Today the words with which the angel reassured the frightened hearts of the women on Easter morning are addressed to all: "Do not be afraid.... He is not here; for he has risen" (Mt 28:5–6). Jesus is risen, and he gives us peace; he himself is peace. For this reason, the Church repeats insistently: "Christ is risen—*Christós anésti*." Let the people of the third millennium not be afraid to open their hearts to him. His Gospel totally quenches the thirst for peace and happiness that is found in every human heart. Christ is now alive, and he walks with us. What an immense mystery of love!

"Urbi et Orbi" Message, April 16, 2006

Our Hope Is Trustworthy

According to the Christian faith, "redemption"—salvation—is not simply a given. Redemption is offered to us in the sense that we have been given hope, trustworthy hope, by virtue of which we can face our present: the present, even if it is arduous, can be lived and accepted if it leads toward a goal, if we can be sure of this goal, and if this goal is great enough to justify the effort of the journey.

Encyclical Letter Spe salvi, *November 30, 2007, no. 1*

Listening to a Firm Hope

The only "certain" and "reliable" hope (cf. *Spe salvi*, no. 1) is founded on God. History has demonstrated the absurdities to which man descends when he excludes God from the horizon of his choices and actions and how hard it is to build a society inspired by the values of goodness, justice, and fraternity, because man is free and his freedom remains fragile. Freedom has constantly to be won over for the cause of good, and the arduous search for the "right way to order human affairs" is a task that belongs to all generations (cf. ibid., nos. 24–25). That, dear friends, is why our first reason for being here is to listen, to listen for a word that will show us the way that leads to hope; indeed, we are listening to the only word that can give us firm hope, because it is God's word.

Homily at the Holy Mass, Brno, Czech Republic, September 27, 2009

Christ Is Our Hope in an Alienated World

In present-day society, many forms of poverty are born from isolation, from being unloved, from the rejection of God, and from a deep-seated tragic closure in man who believes himself to be self-sufficient, or else merely an insignificant and transient datum; in this world of ours that is alienated "when too much trust is placed in merely human projects" (*Caritas in veritate*, no. 53), only Christ can be our certain hope. This is the message that we Christians are called to spread every day, through our witness....

Jesus never abandons his friends. He assures us of his help, because nothing can be done without him, but at the same time, he asks everyone to make a personal commitment to spread his universal message of love and peace.

Homily at the Holy Mass, Brno, Czech Republic, September 27, 2009

God's Great Hope Corrects Our Human Hopes

Problems are not lacking in the Church and in the world, as well as in the daily life of families, but thanks be to God our hope is not based on improbable predictions or financial forecasts, however important these may be. Our hope is in God, not in the sense of a generic religiosity or a fatalism cloaked in faith. We trust in God, who revealed completely and definitively in Jesus Christ his desire to be with man, to share in our history, to guide us all to his Kingdom of love and life. And this great hope enlivens and at times corrects our human hopes.

Angelus, January 3, 2010

Christ Illuminates the Darkest Nights

In spite of all, there is good in the world, and this good is bound to win, thanks be to God, the God of Jesus Christ, who was born, died, and rose again. At times, of course, it is hard to understand this profound reality, because evil is noisier than goodness. An atrocious murder, widespread violence, grave forms of injustice hit the headlines, whereas acts of love and service, the daily effort sustained with fidelity and patience, are often left in the dark; they pass unnoticed. For this reason, too, we cannot stop at reading the news if we wish to understand the world and life; we must be able to pause in silence, in meditation, in calm, prolonged reflection; we must know how to stop and think. In this way, our mind can find healing from the inevitable wounds of daily life; it can penetrate the events that occur in our life and in the world and can attain that wisdom which makes it possible to see things with new eyes. It is above all in the recollection of the conscience that God speaks to us, so that we can learn to evaluate truthfully our own actions and also the evil present within us and around us. In this way, we are able to start out afresh on a journey of conversion that makes us wiser and better people, more capable of generating solidarity and communion and of overcoming evil with good. Christians are people of hope, even and above all when they face the darkness that often exists in the world and has nothing to do with God's plan but is the result of the erroneous choices of human beings, for Christians know that the power of faith can move mountains (cf. Mt 17:20). The Lord can illuminate even the thickest darkness.

Homily at the First Vespers for the Solemnity of Mary, Mother of God, December 31, 2012

All Is Grace,
Not Something "I Did"

Meditations on Holiness

If We Love, We Enter into Holiness

From eternity we have been in God's sight, and he decided to save us. The content of this calling is our "holiness", a great word. Holiness is participation in the purity of the Divine Being. But we know that God is love. Participating in divine purity, therefore, means participating in the "charity" of God, conforming ourselves to God, who is "charity". "God is love" (1 Jn 4:8, 16): this is the comforting truth that also makes us understand that "holiness" is not a reality remote from our own lives, but we enter into the mystery of "holiness" to the extent that we can become people who love together with God. Thus, the *agape* becomes our daily reality. We are therefore transferred to the sacred and vital horizon of God himself.

General Audience, July 6, 2005

Holiness: Putting Nothing before Christ

The secret of holiness is friendship with Christ and faithful obedience to his will. Saint Ambrose said: "Christ is everything for us"; and Saint Benedict warned against putting anything before the love of Christ. May Christ be everything for you.... Be the first to offer him what is most precious to you, as Pope John Paul II suggested in his message for the Twentieth World Youth Day: the gold of your freedom, the incense of your ardent prayer, the myrrh of your most profound affection (cf. no. 4).

Address to the Seminarians of Cologne, August 19, 2005

The Saints Are the Picture Book of the Gospel

The Magi from the East are just the first in a long procession of men and women who have constantly tried to gaze upon God's star in their lives, going in search of the God who has drawn close to us and shows us the way.

It is the great multitude of the saints—both known and unknown—in whose lives the Lord has opened up the Gospel before us and turned over the pages; he has done this throughout history, and he still does so today. In their lives, as if in a great picture book, the riches of the Gospel are revealed. They are the shining path that God himself has traced throughout history and is still tracing today.

Address at the World Youth Day Vigil, Cologne, August 20, 2005

Holiness Breaks the Barrier of Death

New life, received in Baptism, is not subject to corruption and the power of death. For those who live in Christ, death is the passage from the earthly pilgrimage to the Heavenly Homeland, where the Father welcomes all his children "from every nation, from all tribes and peoples and tongues", as we read today in the Book of Revelation (7:9). For this reason, it is very significant and appropriate that after the Solemnity of All Saints, the Liturgy tomorrow has us celebrate the Commemoration of all the Faithful Departed. The "communion of saints", which we profess in the Creed, is a reality that is constructed here below, but it is fully made manifest when we will see God "as he is" (1 Jn 3:2). It is the reality of a family bound together by a deep bond of spiritual solidarity that unites the faithful departed to those who are pilgrims in the world. It is a mysterious but real bond, nourished by prayer and participation in the Sacrament of the Eucharist. In the Mystical Body of Christ, the souls of the faithful meet, overcoming the obstacle of death; they pray for one another, carrying out in charity an intimate exchange of gifts. In this dimension of faith, one understands the practice of offering prayers of suffrage for the dead, especially in the Sacrament of the Eucharist,

the memorial of Christ's Passover that opened to
believers the passage to eternal life.

Angelus, November 1, 2005

The Saints Are Not a Caste, but a Crowd

Today we contemplate the mystery of the communion of saints in Heaven and on earth. We are not alone, but surrounded by a great cloud of witnesses. With them, we form the Body of Christ; with them, we are children of God; with them, we are made saints through the Holy Spirit. Let the heavens be glad and the earth rejoice! The glorious host of saints intercedes for us with the Lord. They accompany us in our journey toward the Kingdom. They spur us to keep our eyes fixed on the Lord Jesus, who will come in glory with his saints. . . .

The saints are not a small caste of chosen souls, but an innumerable crowd to which the Liturgy urges us to raise our eyes. This multitude includes not only the officially recognized saints but also the baptized of every epoch and nation who sought to carry out the divine will faithfully and lovingly. We are unacquainted with the faces and even the names of many of them, but with the eyes of faith we see them shine in God's firmament like glorious stars.

Address and Homily at the Holy Mass, Solemnity of All Saints, November 1, 2006

Fidelity and Courage:
The Main Roads to Sanctity

In our day, is holiness still relevant? Or is it now considered unattractive and unimportant? Do we not place more value today on worldly success and glory? Yet how long does earthly success last, and what value does it have?

The last century . . . saw the fall of a number of powerful figures who had apparently risen to almost unattainable heights. Suddenly they found themselves stripped of their power. Those who denied and continue to deny God, and in consequence have no respect for man, appear to have a comfortable life and to be materially successful. Yet one need only scratch the surface to realize how sad and unfulfilled these people are. Only those who maintain in their hearts a holy "fear of God" can also put their trust in man and spend their lives building a more just and fraternal world. Today there is a need for believers with credibility who are ready to spread in every area of society the Christian principles and ideals by which their action is inspired. This is holiness, the universal vocation of all the baptized, which motivates people to carry out their duty with fidelity and courage, looking not to their own selfish interests but to the common good, seeking God's will at every moment.

Homily at the Holy Mass, Memorial of Saint Wenceslas, Stará Boleslav, Czech Republic, September 28, 2009

Holiness Is Not a Matter of Appearances

The true value of human life is not measured merely in terms of material goods and transient interests, because it is not material goods that quench the profound thirst for meaning and happiness in the heart of every person. This is why Jesus does not hesitate to propose to his disciples the "narrow" path of holiness: "Whoever loses his life for my sake will find it" (Mt 16:25). And he resolutely repeats to us this morning: "If any man would come after me, let him deny himself and take up his cross and follow me" (Mt 16:24). Without doubt, this is hard language, difficult to accept and put into practice, but the testimony of the saints assures us that it is possible for all who trust and entrust themselves to Christ. Their example encourages those who call themselves Christian to be credible, that is, consistent with the principles and the faith that they profess. It is not enough to appear good and honest: one must truly be so. And the good and honest person is one who does not obscure God's light with his own ego, does not put himself forward, but allows God to shine through.

Homily at the Holy Mass, Memorial of Saint Wenceslas, Stará Boleslav, Czech Republic, September 28, 2009

Everything Has Been Given to Us

All that is essential in our existence was bestowed upon us without our contribution. The fact that I am alive does not depend on me. The fact that there were people who introduced me to life, who taught me what it means to love and to be loved, who handed down the faith to me and opened my eyes to God: all this is grace; it was not something "I did". We would not have been able to do anything on our own had we not been granted to do so. God always anticipates our needs, and in every individual life there is a beauty and goodness that we can easily recognize as his grace, as a ray of the light of his goodness. For this reason, we must be attentive; we must always keep open our "inner eyes", the eyes of our heart. And if we learn to know God in his infinite goodness, then we shall be able to see in our lives with wonder, like the saints, the signs of that God who is always close to us, who is always good to us, who says: "Have faith in me!"

Homily at the Holy Mass, Sulmona, Italy, July 4, 2010

Through Prayer, the Saints Become Creative

Faith and prayer do not solve problems but rather enable us to face them with fresh enlightenment and strength, in a way that is worthy of the human being and also more serenely and effectively. If we look at the history of the Church, we see that it is peopled by a wealth of saints and blesseds who, precisely by starting from an intense and constant dialogue with God, illumined by faith, were able to find creative, ever new solutions to respond to practical human needs in all the centuries: health, education, work, etc. Their entrepreneurial character was motivated by the Holy Spirit and by a strong and generous love for their brethren, especially for the weakest and most underprivileged.

Meeting with Young People, Sulmona, Italy, July 4, 2010

Holiness: Not Extraordinary Deeds, but Union with Christ

The saints expressed in various ways the powerful and transforming presence of the Risen One. They let Jesus so totally overwhelm their life that they could say with Saint Paul: "It is no longer I who live, but Christ who lives in me" (Gal 2:20). Following their example, seeking their intercession, entering into communion with them, "brings us closer to Christ, so our companionship with the saints joins us to Christ, from whom as from their fountain and head issue every grace and the life of the People of God itself" (*Lumen gentium*, no. 50)....

What does it mean to be holy? Who is called to be holy? We are often led to think that holiness is a goal reserved for a few elect. Saint Paul, instead, speaks of God's great plan and says: "Even as he [God] chose us in him [Christ] before the foundation of the world, that we should be holy and blameless before him" (Eph 1:4). And he was speaking about all of us. At the center of the divine plan is Christ, in whom God shows his face, in accord with the favor of his will. The Mystery hidden in the centuries is revealed in its fullness in the Word made flesh....

Holiness, the fullness of Christian life, does not consist in carrying out extraordinary enterprises but in being united with Christ, in living his mysteries, in making our own his example, his thoughts, his behavior. The measure of holiness stems from the stature that Christ achieves in us, inasmuch as with the power of the Holy Spirit, we model our whole life on his.

General Audience, April 13, 2011

We Don't Make Ourselves Holy; God Does

How can we take the path to holiness, in order to respond to this call? Can I do this on my own initiative? The answer is clear. A holy life is not primarily the result of our efforts, of our actions, because it is God, the three times Holy (cf. Is 6:3), who sanctifies us; it is the Holy Spirit's action that enlivens us from within; it is the very life of the Risen Christ that is communicated to us and that transforms us. . . .

How can it happen that our manner of thinking and our actions become thinking and action with Christ and of Christ? What is the soul of holiness? . . .

It seems to me that this is the true simplicity and greatness of a life of holiness: the encounter with the Risen One on Sunday; contact with God at the beginning and at the end of the day; following, in decisions, the "signposts" that God has communicated to us, which are but forms of charity.

"Hence the true disciple of Christ is marked by love both of God and of neighbor" (*Lumen gentium*, no. 42). This is the true simplicity, greatness, and depth of Christian life, of being holy. . . .

We are all called to holiness: it is the very measure of Christian living. . . .

I would like to ask all to open themselves to the action of the Holy Spirit, who transforms our life, to be, we too, as small pieces in the great mosaic of holiness that God continues to create in history, so that the face of Christ may shine out in the fullness of its splendor. Let us not be afraid to aim high, for God's heights; let us not be afraid that God will ask too much of us, but let ourselves be guided by his Word in every daily action, even when we feel poor, inadequate, sinners. It will be he who transforms us in accordance with his love.

General Audience, April 13, 2011

We Find Life Only in Giving It

Meditations on Truth and Freedom

To Live Well Is to Live according to the Truth

Love is not dependence but a gift that makes us live. The freedom of a human being is the freedom of a limited being and, therefore, is itself limited. We can possess it only as a shared freedom, in the communion of freedom: only if we live in the right way, with one another and for one another, can freedom develop. We live in the right way if we live in accordance with the truth of our being, and that is in accordance with God's will. For God's will is not a law for man imposed from the outside, a law that constrains him, but the intrinsic measure of his nature, a measure that is engraved within him and makes him the image of God, hence, a free creature. If we live in opposition to love and against the truth—in opposition to God—then we destroy one another and destroy the world. Then we do not find life but act in the interests of death.

Homily at the Holy Mass, Immaculate Conception, December 8, 2005

Man Becomes Truly Himself by Becoming Divine

If we look ... at the world that surrounds us, we can see that ... evil is always poisonous, does not uplift human beings but degrades and humiliates them. It does not make them any the greater, purer, or wealthier, but harms and belittles them. This is something we should indeed learn ...: the person who abandons himself totally in God's hands does not become God's puppet, a boring "yes man"; he does not lose his freedom. Only the person who entrusts himself totally to God finds true freedom, the great, creative immensity of the freedom of good. The person who turns to God does not become smaller but greater, for through God and with God he becomes great, he becomes divine, he becomes truly himself. The person who puts himself in God's hands does not distance himself from others, withdrawing into his private salvation; on the contrary, it is only then that his heart truly awakens and he becomes a sensitive—and thus benevolent and open—person.

Homily at the Holy Mass, Immaculate Conception, December 8, 2005

Truth Spreads through Nature

Those who are committed to truth cannot fail to reject the law of might, which is based on a lie and has so frequently marked human history, nationally and internationally, with tragedy. The lie often parades itself as truth, but in reality it is always selective and tendentious, selfishly designed to manipulate people and finally subject them. Political systems of the past, but not only the past, offer a bitter illustration of this. Set against this, there are truth and truthfulness, which lead to encounter with the other, to recognition and understanding: through the splendor that distinguishes it—the *splendor veritatis*—truth cannot fail to spread; and the love of truth is intrinsically directed toward just and impartial understanding and rapprochement, whatever difficulties there may be.

Address to the Diplomatic Corps Accredited to the Holy See, January 9, 2006

No Competition between Reason and Faith

The Church welcomes with joy the authentic break-throughs of human knowledge and recognizes that evangelization also demands a proper grasp of the horizons and the challenges that modern knowledge is unfolding. In fact, the great progress of scientific knowledge that we saw during the last century has helped us understand the mystery of creation better and has profoundly marked the awareness of all peoples. However, scientific advances have sometimes been so rapid as to make it very difficult to discern whether they are compatible with the truths about man and the world that God has revealed. At times, certain assertions of scientific knowledge have even been opposed to these truths. This may have given rise to a certain confusion among the faithful and may also have made the proclamation and acceptance of the Gospel difficult. Consequently, every study that aims to deepen the knowledge of the truths discovered by reason is vitally important, in the certainty that there is no "competition of any kind between reason and faith" (*Fides et ratio*, no. 17).

We must have no fears about facing this challenge: Jesus Christ is indeed the Lord of all creation and of all history. The believer knows well that "all things were created through him and for him . . . and in him all things hold together" (Col 1:16–17). By continually deepening our knowledge of Christ, the center of the cosmos, and of history, we can show the men and women of our time that faith in him is important for humanity's future: indeed, it is the accomplishment of all that is authentically human. Only in this perspective will we be able to give convincing answers to the person who is searching. This commitment is crucially important for the proclamation and transmission of the faith in the contemporary world. Today, in fact, the task of evangelizing is an urgent priority and demands equal commitment. The dialogue between faith and reason, religion and science, makes it possible not only to show people of our time the reasonableness of faith in God as effectively and convincingly as possible but also to demonstrate that the definitive fulfillment of every authentic human aspiration rests in Jesus Christ. In this regard, a serious evangelizing effort cannot ignore the questions that arise also from today's scientific and philosophical discoveries.

Address at the Plenary Assembly of the Congregation for the Doctrine of the Faith, February 10, 2006

Freedom Is Gift, Not Possession

Life and freedom: these are the things for which we all yearn. But what is this—where and how do we find "life"? I think that the vast majority of people spontaneously have the same concept of life as the Prodigal Son of the Gospel. He had his share of the patrimony given to him and then felt free; in the end, what he wanted was no longer to live burdened by the duties of home, but just to live. He wanted everything that life can offer. He wanted to enjoy it to the full—living, only living, immersed in life's abundance, missing none of all the valuable things it can offer. In the end, he found himself caring for pigs and even envying those animals, so empty and useless had his life become. And even his freedom was proving useless. When all that people want from life is to take possession of it, it becomes ever emptier and poorer; it is easy to end up seeking refuge in drugs, in the great deception. And doubts surface as to whether, in the end, life is truly a good. No, we do not find life in this way. Jesus' words about life in abundance are found in the Good Shepherd discourse. His words are set in a double context. Concerning the shepherd, Jesus tells us that he lays down his life. "No one takes [my life] from me, but I lay it down of my own accord" (Jn 10:18). It is only in giving life that it is found; life is not found by seeking to possess it. This is what we must learn from Christ; and the Holy Spirit teaches us that it is a pure gift, that it is God's gift of himself. The more one gives one's life for others, for goodness itself, the more abundantly the river of life flows.

Homily at the Holy Mass, Pentecost, Meeting with the Ecclesial Movements and New Communities, June 3, 2006

Human Freedom Is Always a Shared Freedom

There is no doubt that we are living in a moment of extraordinary development in the human capacity to decipher the rules and structures of matter and in the consequent dominion of man over nature. We all see the great advantages of this progress, and we see more and more clearly the threat of the destruction of nature by what we do. There is another less visible danger, but no less disturbing: the method that permits us to know ever more deeply the rational structures of matter makes us ever less capable of perceiving the source of this rationality, creative Reason. The capacity to see the laws of material being makes us incapable of seeing the ethical message contained in being, a message that tradition calls *lex naturalis*, natural moral law. This word for many today is almost incomprehensible due to a concept of nature that is no longer metaphysical, but only empirical. The fact that nature, being itself, is no longer a transparent moral message creates a sense of disorientation that renders the choices of daily life precarious and uncertain. Naturally, the disorientation strikes in a particular way the younger generations, who must in this context find the fundamental choices for their life.

It is precisely in the light of this contestation that all the urgency of the necessity to reflect upon the theme of natural law and to rediscover its truth common to all men appears. The said law, to which the Apostle Paul refers (cf. Rom 2:14–15), is written on the heart of man and is consequently, even today, accessible. This law has as its first and general principle "to do good and to avoid evil". This is a truth that by its very evidence immediately imposes itself on everyone. From it flows the other more particular principles that regulate ethical justice on the rights and duties of everyone. So does the principle of respect for *human life* from its conception to its natural end, because this good of life is not man's property but the free gift of God. Besides this is the duty *to seek the truth* as the necessary presupposition of every authentic personal maturation. Another fundamental application of the subject is *freedom*. Yet taking into account the fact that human freedom is always a freedom shared with others, it is clear that the harmony of freedom can be found only in what is common to all: the truth of the human being, the fundamental message of being itself, the very *lex naturalis*. And how can we not mention, on one hand, the demand of *justice* that manifests itself in giving *unicuique suum* and, on the other, the expectation of *solidarity* that nourishes in everyone, especially if he is poor, the hope of the help of the more fortunate? In these values are expressed unbreakable and contingent norms that do not depend on the will of the legislator and not even on the consensus that the State can and must give. They are, in fact, norms that precede any human law: as such, they are not subject to modification by anyone.

Address to the International Congress on Natural Moral Law, February 12, 2007

True Freedom Is More Than the Free Market

There is also something sinister that stems from the fact that freedom and tolerance are so often separated from truth. This is fueled by the notion, widely held today, that there are no absolute truths to guide our lives. Relativism, by indiscriminately giving value to practically everything, has made "experience" all-important. Yet, experiences, detached from any consideration of what is good or true, can lead, not to genuine freedom, but to moral or intellectual confusion, to a lowering of standards, to a loss of self-respect, and even to despair.

Dear friends, life is not governed by chance; it is not random. Your very existence has been willed by God, blessed and given a purpose (cf. Gen 1:28)! Life is not just a succession of events or experiences, helpful though many of them are. It is a search for the true, the good, and the beautiful. It is to this end that we make our choices; it is for this that we exercise our freedom; it is in this—in truth, in goodness, and in beauty—that we find happiness and joy. Do not be fooled by those who see you as just another consumer in a market of undifferentiated possibilities, where choice itself becomes the good, novelty usurps beauty, and subjective experience displaces truth.

Christ offers more! Indeed, he offers everything! Only he who is the Truth can be the Way and hence also the

Life. Thus the "way" that the Apostles brought to the ends of the earth is life in Christ. This is the life of the Church. And the entrance to this life, to the Christian way, is Baptism.

Address to Young People, World Youth Day, Sydney, July 17, 2008

The Absolute "I" Is Not Freedom

What is freedom? How can we be free? Saint Paul helps us to understand this complicated reality that is freedom, inserting this concept into fundamentally anthropological and theological context. He says: "Do not use your freedom as an opportunity for the flesh, but through love be servants of one another" (Gal 5:13). The Rector has already told us that the "flesh" is not the body, but, in the language of Saint Paul, "flesh" is an expression of the absolutization of self, of the self that wants to be all and to take all for its own. The absolute "I" who depends on nothing and on no one seems to possess freedom truly and definitively. I am free if I depend on no one, if I can do anything I want. But exactly this absolutization of the "I" is "flesh", that is, a degradation of man. It is not the conquest of freedom: libertinism is not freedom but rather freedom's failure.

And Paul dares to propose a strong paradox: "Through love be servants" (in Greek: *douléuete*). In other words, freedom, paradoxically, is achieved in service. We become free if we become servants of one another. And so Paul places the whole matter of freedom in the light of the truth of man. To reduce oneself to flesh, seemingly elevating oneself to divine status—"I alone am the man"—leads to deception. Because in reality, it is not so: man is not an absolute, as if the "I" can isolate itself and behave only according to its own will. It is contrary to the truth of our being. Our truth is that above all we are creatures, creatures of God, and we live in relationship with the Creator. We are relational beings. And only by accepting our relationality can we enter into the truth; otherwise we fall into deception, and in it, in the end, we destroy ourselves.

Address to the Roman Major Seminary, February 20, 2009

Truth Never Abandons Us

Charity in truth, to which Jesus Christ bore witness by his earthly life and especially by his death and Resurrection, is the principal driving force behind the authentic development of every person and of all humanity. Love—*caritas*—is an extraordinary force that leads people to opt for courageous and generous engagement in the field of justice and peace. It is a force that has its origin in God, Eternal Love and Absolute Truth. Each person finds his good by adherence to God's plan for him, in order to realize it fully: in this plan, he finds his truth, and through adherence to this truth he becomes free (cf. Jn 8:32). To defend the truth, to articulate it with humility and conviction, and to bear witness to it in life are therefore exacting and indispensable forms of charity. Charity, in fact, "rejoices in the [truth]" (1 Cor 13:6). All people feel the interior impulse to love authentically: love and truth never abandon them completely, because these are the vocation planted by God in the heart and mind of every man. The search for love and truth is purified and liberated by Jesus Christ from the impoverishment that our humanity brings to it, and he reveals to us in all its fullness the initiative of love and the plan for true life that God has prepared for us. In Christ, *charity in truth* becomes the face of his Person, a vocation for us to love our brothers and sisters in the truth of his plan. Indeed, he himself is the Truth (cf. Jn 14:6).

Encyclical Letter Caritas in veritate, *June 29, 2009*

We Are Free, Because We Are Capable of Seeking the Truth

There are many who, believing themselves to be gods, believe they need no roots or foundations other than themselves. They take it upon themselves to decide what is true or not, what is good and evil, what is just and unjust; who should live and who can be sacrificed in the interests of other preferences; leaving each step to chance, with no clear path, letting themselves be led by the whim of each moment. These temptations are always lying in wait. It is important not to give in to them, because, in reality, they lead to something so evanescent, like an existence with no horizons, a liberty without God. We, on the other hand, know well that we have been created free, in the image of God, precisely so that we might be in the forefront of the search for truth and goodness, responsible for our actions, not mere blind executives, but creative co-workers in the task of cultivating and beautifying the work of creation. God is looking for a responsible interlocutor, someone who can dialogue with him and love him. Through Christ, we can truly succeed, and, established in him, we give wings to our freedom. Is this not the great reason for our joy? Isn't this the firm ground upon which to build the civilization of love and life, capable of humanizing all of us?

Address to Young People, World Youth Day, Madrid, August 18, 2011

Loved, Therefore Happy

Meditations on Joy

That the Gospel May Reach the World!

[In the Church,] we do not work, as many say, to defend a power. We do not have a worldly, secular power. We do not work for prestige, nor do we work to expand a business or the like. In reality, we work so that the pathways of the world are opened to Christ. The purpose of all our work, with all its ramifications, is actually ultimately so that his Gospel—as well as the joy of redemption—may reach the world. In this sense, even in the little duties of each day that appear to lack luster, we do ... the best we can to cooperate with the Truth, that is, with Christ in his working in the world, so that the world truly becomes the Kingdom of God.

Address to the Staff of the Vatican Secretariat of State, May 21, 2005

True Joy Is Not Pleasure

Suffering, in various forms, is a necessary part of our lives. I would call this a noble suffering. Once again, it is necessary to make it clear that pleasure is not everything. May Christianity give us joy, just as love gives joy. But love is always also a renunciation of self. The Lord himself has given us the formula of what love is: those who lose themselves find themselves; those who spare or save themselves are lost.

It is always an "exodus", hence, painful. True joy is something different from pleasure; joy grows and continues to mature in suffering, in communion with the Cross of Christ. It is here alone that the true joy of faith is born, from which even they are not excluded if they learn to accept their suffering in communion with that of Christ.

Meeting with the Diocesan Clergy of Aosta, Italy, July 25, 2005

Discovering the Faith, We Receive Joy

Anyone who has discovered Christ must lead others to him. A great joy cannot be kept to oneself. It has to be passed on. In vast areas of the world today, there is a strange forgetfulness of God. It seems as if everything would be just the same even without him. But at the same time, there is a feeling of frustration, a sense of dissatisfaction with everyone and everything. People tend to exclaim: "This cannot be what life is about!" Indeed not. And so, together with forgetfulness of God, there is a kind of new explosion of religion. I have no wish to discredit all the manifestations of this phenomenon. There may be sincere joy in the discovery. But to tell the truth, religion often becomes almost a consumer product. People choose what they like, and some are even able to make a profit from it. But religion sought on a do-it-yourself basis cannot ultimately help us. It may be comfortable, but at times of crisis we are left to ourselves. Help people to discover the true star that points out the way to us: Jesus Christ! Let us seek to know him better and better, so as to be able to guide others to him with conviction. This is why love for Sacred Scripture is so important, and in consequence, it is important to know the faith of the Church, which opens up for us the meaning of Scripture. It is the Holy

Spirit who guides the Church as her faith grows, causing her to enter ever more deeply into the truth (cf. Jn 16:13).

Homily at the Holy Mass, World Youth Day, Cologne, August 21, 2005

The Explosion of Good Overcomes Evil

The Church is the great family through which God creates a space of communion and unity between every continent, culture, and race, a family vaster than the world that knows limits and boundaries; a "great band of pilgrims", so to speak, who walk together with Christ, guided by him, the bright star that illumines history. Jesus makes himself our traveling companion in the Eucharist, and the Eucharist ... brings about "nuclear fission" in the very heart of being. Only this innermost explosion of good that overcomes evil can give life to other transformations that are necessary to change the world. May Jesus, the face of the merciful Lord for every person, continue to light our way, like the star that guided the Magi, and fill us with his joy.

General Audience, August 24, 2005

To Lack Joy Is to Lack the Essential

The people who do not go to church do not know that it is precisely Jesus they are missing. But they feel that something is missing in their lives. If God is absent from my life, if Jesus is absent from my life, I'm missing a guide, an essential friend. I'm also missing a joy that is important for my life, the strength to grow as a man, to overcome my vices and mature as a human being. So even if we cannot immediately see the effects of being with Jesus and of going to Communion, with the passing of the weeks and years, we feel more and more keenly the absence of God, the absence of Jesus. It is a fundamental and destructive incompleteness. I could easily speak of countries where atheism has prevailed for years: how not only souls are destroyed, but also the earth. In this way, we can see that it is important, and I would say fundamental, to be nourished by Jesus in Communion. It is he who gives us enlightenment, offers us guidance for our lives, a guidance that we need.

Meeting with Children after Their First Communion, October 15, 2005

God's Nearness Brings Joy to the Depths

The New Testament is truly "Gospel", the "Good News" that brings us joy. God is not remote from us, unknown, enigmatic, or perhaps dangerous. God is close to us, so close that he makes himself a child, and we can talk to this God like a loved one or a friend [*possiamo dare del "tu" a questo Dio*].

It was the Greek world above all that grasped this innovation, that felt this joy deeply, for it had been unclear to the Greeks whether there was a good God, a wicked God, or simply no God. Religion at that time spoke to them of so many divinities: therefore, they had felt they were surrounded by very different divinities that were opposed to one another; thus, they were afraid that if they did something for one of these divinities, another might be offended and seek revenge. So it was that they lived in a world of fear, surrounded by dangerous demons, never knowing how to save themselves from these forces in conflict with one another. It was a world of fear, a dark world. Then they heard: "Rejoice, these demons are nothing; the true God exists and this true God is good, he loves us, he knows us, he is with us, with us even to the point that he took on flesh!" This is the great joy that Christianity proclaims. Knowing this God is truly "Good News", a word of redemption.

Homily at the Holy Mass, Church of Santa Maria Consolatrice, Rome, December 18, 2005

Gladness Comes from the Freedom God Offers Us

Perhaps we Catholics who have always known it are no longer surprised and no longer feel this liberating joy keenly. However, if we look at today's world where God is absent, we cannot but note that it is also dominated by fears and uncertainties: Is it good to be a person or not? Is it good to be alive or not? Is it truly a good to exist? Or might everything be negative? And they really live in a dark world; they need anaesthetics to be able to live. Thus, the words: "Rejoice, because God is with you, he is with us," are words that truly open a new epoch. Dear friends, with an act of faith we must once again accept and understand in the depths of our hearts this liberating word: "Rejoice!"

We cannot keep solely for ourselves this joy that we have received; joy must always be shared. Joy must be communicated. Mary went without delay to communicate her joy to her cousin Elizabeth. And ever since her Assumption into Heaven, she has showered joy upon the whole world; she has become the great Consoler: our Mother who communicates joy, trust, and kindness and also invites us to spread joy. This is the real commitment of Advent: to bring joy to others. Joy is the true gift of Christmas, not expensive presents that demand time and money. We can transmit this joy simply: with a smile, with a kind gesture, with some small help, with forgiveness. Let us give this joy, and the joy given will be returned to us. Let us seek in particular to communicate the deepest joy, that of knowing God in Christ. Let us pray that this presence of God's liberating joy will shine out in our lives.

Homily at the Holy Mass, Church of Santa Maria Consolatrice, Rome, December 18, 2005

Loved by God: The Source of Happiness

The source of Christian joy is the certainty of being loved by God, loved personally by our Creator, by the One who holds the entire universe in his hands and loves each one of us and the whole great human family with a passionate and faithful love, a love greater than our infidelities and sins, a love that forgives. This love "is so great that it turns God against himself", as appears definitively in the mystery of the Cross: "So great is God's love for man that by becoming man he follows him even into death, and so reconciles justice and love" (*Deus caritas est*, no. 10).

Dear brothers and sisters, this certitude and this joy of being loved by God must be conveyed in some palpable and practical way to each one of us, and especially to the young generations who are entering the world of faith. In other words: Jesus said he was the "Way" that leads to the Father, as well as the "Truth" and the "Life" (cf. Jn 14:5–7). Thus, the question is, How can our children and young people, practically and existentially, find in him this path of salvation and joy? This is precisely the great mission for which the Church—as the family of God and the company of friends into which we are already integrated with Baptism as tiny children—exists and in which our faith and joy and the certainty of being loved by the Lord must grow. It is therefore indispensable—and this is the task entrusted to Christian families, priests, catechists, and educators; to young people themselves among their peers; to our parishes, associations, and movements; and lastly to the entire diocesan community—that the new generations experience the Church as a company of friends who are truly dependable and close in all life's moments and circumstances, whether joyful and gratifying or arduous and obscure; as a company that will never fail us, not even in death, for it carries within it the promise of eternity.

Address at the Ecclesial Convention of the Diocese of Rome, June 5, 2006